THE CHRISTIAN PARENT'S GUIDE TO SEX EDUCATION FOR 8-to-12-year Olds:

How To Teach Your Child About Sex, Puberty, Dating and Intimacy the Godly Way, in the 21st Century.

BY

Brenna K. Wynne

TABLE OF CONTENTS

Get Access to More Parenting Resources

Scan the Code Below!

INTRODUCTION

Navigating the Talk in a Hypersexualized Age

"Well, that was significantly awkward," embarrassed dad Richard sighed, closing 15-year-old son Timmy's bedroom door. Timmy's mom Jen could tell their attempt at "the talk" hadn't gone smoothly by her husband's flushed face and reluctant admission.

"I tried to explain respect for girls and what can happen when hormones run wild, but I basically put my foot in my mouth," Richard said shaking his head.

"It's so hard with today's hookup culture and access to weird stuff online to give them a holy perspective," Jen sympathized. She had suggested they prepare Timmy for the physical and emotional changes adolescence could bring before temptation outpaced prudence. But neither felt adequately equipped to address sexuality from a biblical lens that connected positively with a 21st century teen.

"I wish we had framed intimacy and desire within God's truth back when our son was younger, before R-rated movies and racy songs shaped his imagination," Richard said regretfully. "Now it feels awkward imposing moral arguments out of the blue."

A Common Dilemma

As parents navigating a hypersexualized youth culture where purity seems obsolete, Richard and Jen represent so many families today. We know God beckons our children to live counter-culturally. His timeless truth about sexuality and covenant love hasn't changed. But after generations of liberalizing attitudes, how do we champion God's design amidst profound brokenness?

It's a crucial question because our teens are internalizing worldly sexual ethics whether we discuss it or not. If Christian parents abandon this vital facet of discipleship, secular educators and media eagerly fill the void. And while no family is exempt from stumbles, statistics clearly demonstrate that committed mentoring makes a major difference steering youth toward sexual wholeness.

But where do overwhelmed moms and dads turn when they never experienced that nurturing guardrail themselves? How do we foster age-appropriate conversations before outside influence undermines purity and dignity? My hope is this resource helps spark a movement back to grace-filled sexuality discipleship that bears much fruit in generations to come!

Why This Handbook is Essential Today

The journey writing this handbook began when I found myself bumbling awkwardly as a young parent with two rapidly growing kids and little helpful formation around embodied spirituality in my background. My husband and I knew abstinence mattered and media required monitoring for sexual content. But beyond that we lacked vision or language to nurture holistic understanding of why God created gendered, passionate, creative beings to steward intimacy in covenant relationship.

When questions about bodies, identity and attractions emerged around puberty, we struggled putting disjointed purity pep talks into context of loving community and relationship with Christ. We needed guidance bridging faith and development to frame sexuality conversations through the lens of the gospel story early on.

Thankfully through prayer and counsel from mentors over years, we developed reasonable confidence having ongoing grace-filled chats about God's gift of sexuality through every phase, not just crisis avoidance talks upon dating. We built rapport where our maturing son and daughter knew nothing was off limits, no matter how embarrassing, upsetting or confusing.

While by no means perfect parents, we learned tools critical for navigating sex discipleship amidst today's gender chaos and hookup culture. The fruit of caring community and accountability became evident when pressures arose down the road. Now as our teenagers stand on the cusp of young adulthood, they have firm foundations anchoring their passions and convictions through storms rather than drifting aimlessly into regretted decisions.

Passing the Baton

I still claim no expert wisdom. Yet seeing the blessings of good mentoring in our home, I feel called to pass the baton and pay forward what we've learned. My dream is equipping parents to start early instilling biblical sexuality ethics and have grace to course-correct when cultural current threatens to sweep up wandering hearts.

If this handbook spares just one precious child from scars of abuse or experimentation underage, or seeds redemptive understanding for any prodigal teen, it's served its purpose. If one more marriage thrives with intimacy framed positively like God designed from early on, I'll praise Him for every small contribution this offered.

Friends, we serve families in a radically shifting generation compared to our own upbringing. As disciple-making parents, we cannot neglect empowering kids to embrace God's gift of creative, passionate, dignified embodied love. Let's come alongside navigating sexuality conversations with wisdom and vision grounded in the Anchor of Truth across generations. His purposes for intimacy remain steadfast however far society may drift.

CHAPTER ONE

Laying the Groundwork: Having Those First Talks

As parents, we want to keep our children as innocent as possible. The prospect of having "the talk" with our young children about bodies and sex can be intimidating! But it's critical to start these discussions early, framing sexuality as the beautiful gift that God intended it to be.

My daughter Emma was about 5 years old when she walked in on my husband and me kissing in the kitchen. "Eww, what are you guys doing?" she inquired. "Just showing love!" we exclaimed. This raised more questions about how mothers and fathers' express affection. It was an opportunity to explain how God creates desires in us to be close to our spouses, and it was a tame example!

Such occasions allow us to lay the groundwork for healthy conversations as children grow. From a biblical perspective, sex education begins with small talks about bodies, privacy, and relationships. Don't put off the "big talk" until they're older! Begin with age-appropriate honesty and biblical truth now.

Using Correct Terms for Body Parts

Using anatomically correct names for private body parts from a young age is an important way to lay a healthy foundation. There's no need to use cutesy nicknames or silly slang because God created every part of us. Teach your children to call their genitals by their proper names as soon as they can talk, just as you do for their eyes, nose, toes, and so on.

For females, use the terms "vagina" and "breasts." For boys, use the terms "penis" and "testicles." This provides children with the language necessary to describe their bodies and communicate clearly about any concerns. It also removes any stigma or embarrassment associated with private parts, after all, God created them!

Of course, teach children that these areas are private and should not be discussed in public. However, you can instill healthy values without causing unnecessary shame:

"God created your vagina/penis specifically for you!" He wants us to keep our private parts private and only allow parents or doctors to see them when necessary. Thank you for taking such good care of this priceless gift from God!"

Establishing Privacy and Boundaries

We as parents learn best by modeling. Respect your child's privacy and bodily autonomy beginning at a young age:

a. Ask "Can I come in?" before entering their room or bathing them? "Is it ok if I help clean you?" This model represents agreement.

b. Explain what you need to do for care while maintaining modesty when dressing, bathing, or tending wounds near private areas.

   c. If siblings share a room, teach them to change their clothes privately and to respect their privacy in the bathroom.

   d. Emphasize that bodies are not shameful, but that private parts belong only to that person. They should not be touched by other children.

These examples demonstrate that you value their bodily privacy. Children as young as two can understand the importance of respecting others' bodies and covering their own private parts around others.

According to the Bible, our bodies are temples of the Holy Spirit (1 Corinthians 6:19). Even young children, despite their messy habits, can understand the importance of caring for their "temples" through modesty and privacy. Your actions and reminders should help to reinforce these concepts.

Identifying Trusted Adults

Along with using proper anatomy terminology, teach young children the difference between safe and unsafe touch from others from an early age. Tell them which parts are "private zones" and should not be seen or touched by others. Make a list of "safe" adults with whom they can speak if they have concerns about their bodies or relationships.

"Mommy, Daddy, Grandma, and Pastor Mark are always available to listen if you have any concerns," for example. Doctors and nurses can also see your private parts if necessary to keep your body healthy. However, no one else should be allowed to see or touch your private areas. You can always come to us for assistance!"

Of course, parents should conduct background checks on trusted adults in their lives. Giving children a short list, on the other hand, empowers them to speak up if inappropriate behavior occurs. Proverbs 22:6 says to train children in the way they should go. It is critical to equip them to report abuse today. More on innocence protection in Chapter 6.

Developing Modesty and Respect

Another way to lay a solid foundation is to instill modesty and respect in young children through your example. Small children are literal mimics and concrete thinkers. They tend to repeat what they see and hear rather than what they are told!

If parents are careless with their bodies, their children will be as well. They'll think it's acceptable if you watch crass shows and objectify others. But modeling modest language and behavior teaches them far more than lectures on "saving yourself for marriage" when they're older.

Here are some suggestions for teaching children a healthy respect for God's gift of sexuality:

1. Use caution when speaking and acting in front of children's ears and eyes. Keep crude jokes and language to a minimum.

2. Filtering media choices can help to counteract our hypersexualized culture. Don't watch shows or listen to music that glorifies sex. Explain why a comment or image was offensive.

3. Value character over appearance. Rather than gushing over cute outfits, say, "You were so kind to help Grandpa today!"

4. Show your spouse respect through your words and affection. Keep passionate kissing and hands-on flirting to yourself.

5. Think of your body as a temple, not an object. Don't criticize your appearance in front of children or obsess over flaws.

6. Enforce respectful ways for children to interact with one another. Allow no bottom-patting or "you show me yours; I'll show you mine." Redirect their attention to more constructive play.

According to the Bible, we should "fix our thoughts on what is true, honorable, and right" (Philippians 4:8). When children are young, they are taught proper speech and behavior, which shapes their attitudes as they grow.

Laying a Solid Foundation

I hope these suggestions encourage you to have early conversations with your children about their bodies, privacy, and relationships. There's no need to overwhelm young children with information they're not ready for. However, laying a foundation of biblical truth and healthy respect for children when they are young reaps enormous benefits as they grow.

The world will soon attack their innocence. As Christian parents, we must be deliberate in framing sexuality as the beautiful gift that God intended it to be. When we teach children modesty, discretion, and godly values from a young age, they develop healthy boundaries and respect for their bodies and those of others as they grow.

Things will continue to be awkward at times! However, beginning early helps to frame physical changes in the context of embracing God's design. Stay tuned for more advice on guiding your child into adulthood with a biblical perspective on sexuality.

Question and Answer for Chapter 1

Q: Why do I have to call my private parts special names like "penis" and "vagina"? Can't I use cute nicknames?

A: God carefully designed every part of your body and gave them proper names, like eyes, ears, toes etc. There's no need to use made-up names for body parts God created. Using the right anatomy terms helps you talk clearly about your body as the special gift it is.

Q: Why can't I touch or play with my private parts at the dinner table or in front of other people?

A: Your private parts are just for you, not for public display. Even though God made them good, we keep them private out of respect for ourselves and others. Playing with privates should happen in private spaces like your bedroom or the bath.

Q: Should I be embarrassed or ashamed of my body?

A: Not at all! God said each person He created is wonderfully made (Psalm 139:14). Every part of you is a gift from Him. There's no need to feel ashamed of your body. Just cherish it and take good care of it.

Q: Why do I need to be careful about people seeing me without clothes or touching my private zones?

A: Your body deserves privacy and respect. The parts covered by your swimsuit are private zones that only you or parents and doctors should see or touch if needed. Saying "no" firmly if anyone else tries to see or touch them keeps your body safe and honors how God made you.

Q: Who are trusted adults I can talk to if I have questions or worries about my body?

A: You can always come to me or [other parent] with any concerns. Teachers and our pastor are also safe people you can share worries with. Remember you won't be in trouble - we're here to help you.

CHAPTER TWO

Puberty and Physical Changes

12-year-old Lucy sighed while bra shopping with mom Maria, eyeing all the training bras she wasn't quite ready for. Meanwhile her athletic best friend Leah already wore a B cup after getting her period last year.

"It's not fair!" Lucy complained. "Why do I have the body of a baby but Leah already looks like a woman? I must have done something wrong for God to curse me with delayed puberty."

Seeing her daughter's distress, compassionate mom Maria drew Lucy into a comforting side hug. "I'm so sorry, sweetie. I know the uneven changes can feel really frustrating right now. But I promise you're right on God's schedule."

Crucial Conversations

It was just one of many puberty-sparked meltdowns Maria anticipated navigating during this awkward phase of growth into womanhood. She still remembered her own bumpy adolescent years navigating bodily changes without much guidance. After becoming a Christian in college, Maria wished she had someone interpret this unstoppable transformation through a gospel-shaped lens.

Now as a mom herself, she was determined to normalize her daughter's worries by discussing puberty openly. She longed to plant seeds about embodiment and God's unconditional love that she'd pray would take root spiritually before planet earth's pressures choked them out.

Maria knew she needed to have frank talks about new sensations that management with modesty and self-control. But she first wanted to offer Lucy freedom from shame over developing early, late or differently from the world's ideals...

Walking With Her Daughter

Pausing in the bra aisle after that angst-filled exchange, Maria drew Lucy aside calmly. "Honey, why don't we grab a hot cocoa and chat about this overwhelming stage you're in?" Lucy shrugged and nodded, swiping her sleeve across teary eyes.

Settling into a corner booth with steaming mugs, Maria looked at her hurting little girl with compassion. She reached out to squeeze Lucy's hand gently. "I know it's really hard being in between childhood and womanhood. I remember both wanting to hurry up and slow down growing up too! Every part of God's timing confuses us sometimes."

"But I promise however your body keeps changing this year is normal – you can always come to me when worries pop up. If certain changes tarry awhile, I'm here to listen without judgment. And if new curves or other developments take you by surprise, I'll guide you through."

Maria smiled reassuringly. "The most important thing isn't what starts developing when alongside friends. What matters most is anchoring your worth and identity in Christ. He created you beautifully as His precious daughter, no matter how tall or slim other girls get!"

She squeezed Lucy's hand gently. "My prayer is by talking openly together, you'll learn to receive these changes unfolding as a gift, not a curse! God timed your blossoming into womanhood exactly right. Let me know whenever I can help smooth the road ahead..."

Navigating Puberty with Grace

Puberty is often the most dreaded sex education topic! It's frightening to think that our children are now old enough to learn about periods, wet dreams, and hair in strange places. Even devout Christian parents may feel uncomfortable discussing these subjects.

But keep in mind that our children must learn about adolescence somewhere. As parents, we want our children to receive information from a biblical worldview rather than from peers, the media, or worse.

Puberty can be an emotionally and physically challenging time. But it's also a lovely stage full of wonder, growth, and new ways to honor God with changing bodies. Let us reframe "the puberty talk" in a gospel-centered context to better prepare our children for adulthood.

Timing the Conversation

To begin, when should you initiate "the talk?" Experts recommend starting conversations about a year before puberty. Girls should be between the ages of 8 and 10. For boys aged 9 to 11. Of course, each child develops at his or her own pace. Use your best judgment based on your child's age and spiritual readiness.

You are the most familiar with your child. Determine when introductions to birds and bees will not go over their heads or overwhelm them. Take their questions as cues to start age-appropriate discussions. You should not ignore their concerns, but you should also not overburden young children. Expand on previous discussions about private parts, boundaries, and healthy relationships.

Here are some pointers for properly timing puberty conversations:

a. Ask for wisdom in determining your child's maturity and questions. Ask God for the appropriate words.

b. When they inquire, "Where do babies come from?" Don't be alarmed! Simply respond at their level. There's no need to go into detail just yet.

c. Use teachable moments, such as growth spurts, to explain that puberty is on its way. Assure them that you will guide them through every transition.

d. Have annual checkups with their doctor. Inquire about the onset of puberty and menstruation.

e. Consider your child's surroundings. To stay ahead of misinformation at school, speak up sooner if your classmates are maturing quickly.

f. Explain menstruation to girls several months before they begin their periods. Never let her be caught off guard!

g. Discuss body changes and voice cracking with boys as they begin. Then return to talk about nocturnal emissions once puberty kicks in.

Laying the Groundwork

When you feel the time is right, lay the groundwork by holding an introductory discussion about the upcoming changes. Here are some conversation-starting ideas:

a. Confirm that this is God's perfect timing for their maturation into adults. It's all part of His grand plan.

b. Explain that hormones will send signals to their bodies to begin changing and preparing for childbirth someday.

c. Go over the upcoming changes in advance so they know what to expect. This alleviates anxiety and embarrassment.

d. Encourage them to contact you if they have any questions or concerns. No subject is off-limits! They will learn more from you than from their peers or the media.

e. Inform them that you will discuss fertility and sexuality further in the future. For the time being, just imagine the physical changes that are about to occur.

The goal is to create an open environment in which they know they will be guided through the transformation ahead. Talk frequently and emphasize your willingness to discuss their experiences, fears, and questions.

Changes to Expect

Now for the meat of the matter! Here's a rundown of key puberty changes to anticipate for your son or daughter:

1. **Growth spurts:** Children will begin to grow and gain weight. Appetites will also rise. Explain that this is their body's way of preparing for adulthood by increasing

muscle, body mass, and energy. Stock up on nutritious snacks and adjust your clothing budget accordingly!

2. **Body Hair:** As testosterone levels rise, new hair will grow on the underarms, legs, face, chest, and private parts. Ascertain that shaving products are available. Teach proper grooming techniques for new grooming routines.

3. **Skin Changes:** Oil production increases, which frequently leads to acne. Show them how to incorporate acne washes, spot treatments, and facial scrubs into their hygiene routines. There will be no picking or popping of pimples!

4. **Sweat and Scents:** Be cautious of increased perspiration, body odor, and strong scents emanating from privates. Introduce deodorant, demonstrate proper laundry techniques, and prepare your teen to deal with new "aromas."

For Girls:

Explain what to expect during your first period. Make sure you have enough pads and supplies. Use a calendar to keep track of your cycles. Discuss premenstrual hormone changes such as mood swings, cramping, tender breasts, and so on.

For boys:

Explain typical testosterone-driven responses such as erections and ejaculation while sleeping. Discuss methods for dealing with sexual urges such as cold showers, exercise, and avoiding overstimulation. The goal is not to be ashamed, but to learn self-discipline in the face of new temptations.

These are just a few of the many changes that will occur in the future. Choose appropriate books, websites, or videos to illustrate details that you may be uncomfortable explaining directly. And, as new experiences emerge, always emphasize that you are available for ongoing conversations!

Emotional Reframing

Puberty brings about major emotions associated with changing identities, confidence, and relating to others. As Christian parents, we can help our children navigate turbulence by reframing their emotions through the lens of the gospel.

Moodiness and even depression are frequently caused by fluctuating hormones in girls. Instead of dismissing her emotions as irrational, empathize with her and reframe them:

"I know all of these changes must be exhausting! But when we are weak, God promises us strength. He'll see you through, and I'll be right there with you. This is only the beginning of your journey to becoming a godly woman!"

Boys deal with testosterone surges that drive impulses and aggression they've never known before. However, don't simply tell them to "man up." Validate the challenge, then contextualize the urges:

- "You're maturing into a man endowed with God-given masculine power!" Let's talk about channeling that energy in constructive rather than destructive directions."

- Growth spurts that alternate between clumsiness and new abilities have an effect on self-esteem. Remind them that God created each change for a reason, and that they will eventually master their changing bodies. Remind teens on a regular basis, despite external changes, of their unchanging value and identity in Christ.

Keep an eye out for withdrawals, comparisons, or risky behaviors that indicate difficulty adapting. Seek counseling if necessary to avoid a crisis. However, keep the door open for dealing with difficult emotions.

Sexual Ethics

A significant aspect of "the puberty talk" is sexual ethics. For the first time, soaring hormones elicit sexual curiosity and arousal. As Christian parents, we must frame sexuality as a divine gift intended for marriage.

Discuss appropriate outlets for natural desires, such as exercise, creative endeavors, and wholesome community. Inform people about the dangers of extramarital sex, easy access to pornography, and technology that allows for secretive sin.

Set reasonable limits on technology and unsupervised time with peers. Monitor the use of phones, tablets, and other electronic devices. To prevent access to inappropriate websites and apps, use filters and accountability software.

Maintaining sexual purity should be discussed on a regular basis. Discuss strategies such as avoiding provocative images and focusing mentally on what is honorable. Discuss physical boundaries in dating. Assist teenagers in memorizing scriptures about temptation, such as 1 Corinthians 10:13 and Philippians 4:8.

And reassure your child that if they cross lines, they can always start over with God with repentance and your loving support.

Preparing for Peer Pressure

Puberty brings with it new forms of peer teasing and peer pressure. Explain what might happen:

- Opinions on late or early physical development
- Joking about awkward voice changes
- Body odor, acne, or menstrual leak jokes
- Pressure to date, kiss, send pictures, or engage in sexual activity
- Footloose pals put their parents' values to the test

Prepare your son or daughter to face these challenges with confidence in Christ and their convictions:

- Allow hurtful words to wash over them while clinging to their identity in Christ.
- Seek Christian friends who encourage rather than criticize.
- Refuse to give in to taunts by following your parents' rules.
- Maintain accountability by immediately sharing peer pressures.

A strong Christian community acts as a barrier against conforming to the values of the world. Make sure your teen is involved in youth groups led by godly mentors to reinforce the biblical truths you teach at home.

Embracing Changes

Puberty can be an emotional roller coaster filled with concerns and uncertainty. We must validate children's concerns while encouraging them to view adolescence as a gift from God. Here are some final suggestions for assisting children in flourishing:

- Host period parties and voice change ceremonies. Celebrate their achievements!
- To ease the transition, encourage healthy habits such as rest, nutrition, and exercise.
- Purchase well-fitting clothing and products to assist them in navigating new hygiene requirements comfortably.
- Express your admiration for the godly man or woman they are growing into.
- Remind them frequently that these temporary growing pains lead to wonderful outcomes.
- Watch for teachable moments in which they demonstrate maturity and growth in Christ. Affirm!

With God's guidance and a supportive community, our children can navigate puberty with confidence, purity, and grace. Before you know it, the awkward middle schooler will have matured into a mature young adult ready to live out

God's calling. Puberty necessitates collaboration, but what worthwhile kingdom work does not? Parents, we've got this. Let us do our best to guide the next generation!

Question and Answer for Chapter 2

Q: Why is my body changing so much? It's weird and embarrassing!

A: What you're experiencing is a special time called puberty. It's all part of God's perfect plan. He designed your body to go through these changes as you mature into a man/woman. There's no need to feel embarrassed - growing up is a gift from God!

Q: Do boys and girls go through puberty the same way?

A: Boys and girls both go through a lot of changes in their bodies that prepare them for adulthood. God gives girls the ability to carry babies someday. He gives boys physical strength and features to be fathers and leaders. All the changes are part of His wonderful design.

Q: Why do I sweat so much more lately? I'm so stinky!

A: Sweating more is one of the body changes that happen during puberty. It's because your underarm glands are producing more sweat to help cool your armpits as you grow. Don't feel embarrassed, we'll pick up some deodorant to help you manage new "aromas" as your body matures!

Q: Is it sinful when I start getting new tingly urges and feelings down there?

A: Not at all! God created those desires you're starting to experience. But He does give guidelines to direct those urges wisely as you mature - saving sexual intimacy for marriage is one way to honor Him. Let's talk about how to navigate these new feelings in positive ways.

Q: Why is my chest/bottom growing? I don't like it.

A: Don't worry, developing curves is a normal part of puberty for girls. Your body is changing to prepare for womanhood and being able to nurse babies someday. All these changes are God-designed. Try to embrace them as the gift they are! Let me know if you need help finding well-fitting bras and clothes during this growth spurt.

CHAPTER THREE

Sexual Intimacy in Marriage

"We need to have a little chat about relationships," youth pastor Dave said, turning off the worship music to address his high school small group.

The teens glanced up reluctantly, the guys slouching lower as if to disappear while the girls looked everywhere but his face. Dave understood their nervousness and discomfort with this topic, but he couldn't ignore the rocky romantic dynamics he observed lately among group members.

Just last week Dave consoled sobbing Julie after her boyfriend Luke pressured her to go much further physically than she felt ready for. And some of the cruder boys joked about girls in demeaning sexual ways, oblivious to how uncomfortable Dave noticed their female friends looked.

He knew God cared deeply about how His sons and daughters related across gender. If Dave didn't address some biblical ground rules around pursuing romance, he worried lasting damage might get inflicted on impressionable hearts...

Reframing Perspectives

Clearing his throat, Dave plunged ahead compassionately but without sugarcoating. "I know in today's sexually-charged culture, it's really hard not to get wrapped up in feelings quickly or view others as objects." Glancing around, he made eye contact.

"But as disciples of Jesus, God calls us to a radically different approach to romance - one where we honor Him through pure actions and seeing others' full dignity. I want to help each of you avoid heartbreak or regret by talking through setting some intentional boundaries."

Dave spent the next hour walking through principles like avoiding temptation by not entering dating before mature enough for marriage responsibilities, as well as fleeing lust by directing passion into other creative outlets like sports or music.

He also covered respecting consent rather than pressuring dates, believing the best about one another's intentions unless proven otherwise, and making mental covenants to control thoughts avoiding objectification.

Finally, after reviewing biblical warnings about sexual sin, he ended by praying God would form each teen into the loving, responsible man or woman He designed them to become through obedience over fleeting pleasure...

Equipping a Counter-cultural Ethic

Driving home afterwards, Dave felt he'd delivered crucial guidance for helping this generation reject society's "anything goes sexuality." Yet he recognized that one talk couldn't undo years of normalized vice and toxic stereotypes from media. He resolved to keep finding relatable ways to shape a countercultural ethic around intimacy as an act of devoted love and lifetime commitment rather than casual recreation.

With parents largely reluctant to address evolving dating norms and college fast approaching to challenge convictions; Dave knew his reach remained limited without whole families adopting the baton. But he determined to run his leg faithfully with eyes fixed on the Author and Perfecter of true romance designed not to consume but to bless all who submitted passions to His wise boundaries.

Might other youth leaders join this sacred team relay by maturing teens for marriage rather than inadvertently fueling undirected fires of desire in their care? A movement of grace and truth could spark and perhaps blaze back brighter against darkening skies. An awakening awaited young hearts opened to godly transformation. The choice before them stood vast as eternity.

Honoring Intimacy in Marriage

We must teach our children as Christians that sex is a sacred gift from God intended solely for marriage. Saving sexual intimacy for the wedding night respects God's design and saves a lot of heartache.

Of course, for our hormone-driven teenagers, waiting seems impossible! Premarital purity necessitates the establishment of wise boundaries, constant monitoring, and ongoing discussions about God's plan for passion.

Sex is mentioned early in Scripture, indicating that it is an important part of God's plan:

"That is why a man leaves his father and mother and is united to his wife, and they become one flesh." 2:24 (Genesis)

Marriage establishes a covenant bond, uniting two people as one. Sex completes that union on all levels: physically, emotionally, and spiritually. God clearly established this sexual ethic early on, but cultural pressures continue to test it on a daily basis.

As Christian parents, we must instill in our children that intimacy is only available within marriage. Our youth can walk in purity and avoid the traps that the world sets by God's grace and strong convictions. Let us prepare them to embrace God's lovely design for passion.

Laying a Strong Foundation

Instilling a biblical sexual ethic in teenagers early on is critical to their saving sex for marriage. Conversations about waiting for intimacy should build on years of childhood modesty, purity, and respect.

Review key conversations you've had over the years:

- Using proper names for private parts of the body
- Regarding their bodies as Holy Spirit temples
- Modeling pure speech and behavior after them

- Teaching children to look away from lustful images.
- Talking about inappropriate touching and reporting abuse.
- Keeping an eye on media choices to avoid hypersexualized content.

These discussions promote respect for God's gift of sexuality. Waiting for intimacy in marriage is much easier when you've raised your children to value modesty and purity from the start.

Now, discussions can center on how to apply those values to preserving sexual expression for the sacred union of matrimony. Our teenagers are constantly bombarded with cultural lies about sexuality. We must prepare them to accept God's wise boundaries.

Why Save Sex for Marriage?

Teens today are taught that sexual restraint is antiquated and unhealthy. "Sex is no big deal," say their peers. "Safe sex is smart sex." Pornography makes lust appear natural. But, as followers of Christ, we know that God's way is best, even when it contradicts popular opinion.

But don't simply state, "God forbids it." Explain why He asks us to save intimacy for marriage only:

a. It safeguards the sanctity and meaning of sex as a holy act of oneness. Casual sex desecrates God's plan.

b. It protects you from the agony of broken trust, betrayal, heartbreak, and comparisons that come with premature intimacy.

c. It prevents unintended pregnancy, STDs, and other negative consequences outside of a committed marriage.

d. It allows sex to strengthen an exclusive lifelong bond in the way that God intended.

e. It provides the necessary foundation of friendship, communication, and commitment for success.

f. It reserves intimacy for your spouse only. They have complete ownership of your entire being.

g. It instills self-control and obedience in order to respect God's boundaries.

These advantages make the wait completely worthwhile! And God promises to give us strength and grace when we are tempted. We only need to walk straight in front of Him.

Setting Physical Boundaries

Discuss practical boundaries to maintain purity once the "why" is established. Teens require specific guidelines rather than vague injunctions to "abstain." Please be specific:

- There will be no passionate kissing that arouses strong desires. Simple pecks are acceptable.

- Hands above clothing near private parts.

- No sleeping in the same bed during sleepovers.

- No late nights in bedrooms or cars alone.

- No extended hugs or full-body contact. Quick side hugs are the best.

- There will be no compromising media, sexting, or private web browsing. Make use of filters.

Adapt to your values, but provide specific parameters for intimacy. To combat raging hormones, teenagers require unambiguous rules.

Discuss situations that could test boundaries, such as parties, school dances, dates, and travel trips. Plan ahead of time to stay strong. Give teens vocabulary for saying "no." Play a role in responding to pressures.

And reassure them that if lines are crossed, Christ offers forgiveness and new beginnings!

Managing Sexual Urges

Waiting for marriage entails positive sexual urge management. Teach adolescents:

a. Fill free time with healthy activities and community service. It goes without saying "idle mind is the devil's workshop!"

b. Direct your energy toward vigorous exercise, sports, hobbies, and service.

c. Avoid situations that may lead to temptation.

d. Remove your gaze from provocative images. Concentrate on what is pure. (Philippians 4:8)

e. Make use of internet filters. Keep an eye on the media.

f. Pray and meditate on sexual purity scriptures.

g. Keep yourself busy and engaged to keep your mind from wandering.

Advising them to "just say no" is insufficient. Give people tools to help them redirect their desires and resist lustful thoughts. According to the Bible, "make no provision for the flesh"

(Romans 13:14). Rather than temptation traps, fill their lives with godly influences.

Dating Advice

Teen relationships are unavoidable. Dating opens the door to intimacy, so follow these rules:

a. Early on, group outings are best. Avoid solitary dates away from others.

b. Do activities together that emphasize conversation and sharing rather than physical allure.

c. Communicate clearly about your physical limits in relation to your family's expectations.

d. Avoid situations that may put your boundaries in jeopardy.

e. End relationships that put you under pressure to break rules.

f. Save developing serious intimacy for when marriage is certain.

g. Ensure that spiritual connection takes precedence over physical attraction.

h. Bring your worries, temptations, and pressures to your parents for advice.

Keep a close eye on your teen's relationships. Encourage them to keep things light and friendly until they are ready to marry. Emphasize that true love prioritizes emotional intimacy over physical desires.

Accountability and vigilance are required.

Accountability is critical in our hypersexualized culture. When youth are unsupervised, don't assume purity reigns. Maintain your vigilance:

a. Keep internet access in high-traffic areas rather than bedrooms. Install filtering and monitoring software.

b. Check phones, tablets, and computers for inappropriate content on a regular basis.

c. Always be aware of where they are and who they are with. Make new friends.

d. Pay a visit when your children are at your house. Listen from a different room.

e. Volunteer as an activity chaperone. Collaborate with other trustworthy parents.

f. Communicate with school and youth pastors for assistance and collaboration.

g. Let teens know you're watching them out of love and in their best interests.

In the internet age, privacy must be balanced with prudence. Prevent the enemy of purity, tempting isolation and secrecy. Proactively guard their hearts.

Redemption and Grace

Despite their best efforts, some young people will fall. It is critical to continue the conversation. Assure your adolescent:

a. You are always available to listen and assist without judgment.

b. To those who repent, God offers full redemption (as high as the heavens are above the earth!).

c. There is always the possibility of starting over in Christ.

d. One setback does not define them. Let us learn from this.

e. We will get through this together, and I will always love them.

Then take steps to prevent it from happening again, such as counseling, software filters, ending the relationship, or limiting freedoms.

Bring in pastoral care if necessary. However, show unwavering love while maintaining standards. In God's eyes, we are all precious prodigals!

Refocusing on the Wedding Night

Teens need a positive vision of God's gift of intimacy in marriage after hearing so many warnings. The wedding night should be framed as a holy matrimony celebration, not a humiliating final "base" to cross.

Describe sex as the sweet culmination of two people's sacred covenant before God. Beautifully describe it:

a. The total gift of themselves to each other, with no holds barred.

b. Two souls entwined and cherished by one another.

c. A one-of-a-kind pleasure reserved solely for their spouse.

d. The union of flesh, heart, and spirit.

e. The extraordinary ability to co-create new life.

f. A private pleasure garden for the couple.

g. God blessed them with a holy mystery of oneness.

What a wonderful image for your teen to look forward to rather than fear! And it's now worth every ounce of self-control and patience. Assist them in understanding the richness of intimacy in marriage.

Equipping Purity with Prayer

Of course, maintaining sexual purity is difficult for passionate young people. It is critical to rely on Christ's strength. Here are some pointers:

a. Make frequent requests for pure thoughts and actions. Ask God to keep their hearts safe.

b. Have teens memorize and recite purity scriptures.

c. Quickly confess impure thoughts and behaviors to remove footholds.

d. Allow youth to contact you for emergency prayer when they are confronted with temptation.

e. Introduce them to mentors who demonstrate godly maturity and self-control.

f. Maintain their participation in youth groups for spiritual support and accountability.

g. Ensure that your home is a safe place for you to share your struggles without feeling embarrassed.

Keep a close eye on communication, electronics, and activities. Above all, cover your children in prayer, asking God to cultivate purity in their hearts.

Question and Answer for Chapter 3

Q: Why should I save sex for marriage? Everyone around me is doing it.

A: God designed sex to bond husband and wife in sacred covenant (Genesis 2:24). Waiting shows respect and keeps intimacy safe and special. Let's talk about setting boundaries.

Q: Isn't living together fine if we're committed to marrying someday?

A: Cohabiting often strains commitment instead of cementing it. It also opens the door to sexual temptation. God's way is reserving intimacy for the marriage altar.

Q: How far is too far physically before marriage?

A: Passionate kissing, touching private areas, lingering embraces - these stir intense desires meant for your spouse. Let's talk about saving ultimate intimacy for marriage by avoiding arousal.

Q: What if I mess up sexually? Can I be forgiven?

A: Yes, God offers grace and redemption when we repent (Psalm 103:12). Avoid condemnation but learn positive boundaries moving forward. Accountability helps us resist temptation.

Q: Why save sex for marriage if we'll probably divorce anyway?

A: What a cynical view! But I understand the concern. God's plan for intimacy bonds you and actually cultivates oneness to go the distance. Let's talk about how to prepare for lifelong commitment.

CHAPTER FOUR

Protecting Innocence in a Sexualized Culture

"We need to talk," 15-year-old Justin's dad said gravely, eyebrows knitted. Justin glanced up from his phone distractedly, already on high alert. His dad rarely looked so serious unless someone was in trouble.

"What's up, Dad?" Justin asked cautiously, wondering if a teacher reported his constant tardiness or failing math grade since he'd been up late most nights... browsing things online he knew he shouldn't.

"Well son..." his dad sighed heavily, making fear spike higher in Justin's gut. "The monitoring software on your phone alerted me to some very concerning search history that could lead places no godly young man should wander..."

Unexpected Confrontation

Justin paled realizing he hadn't been as stealthy about deleting those sensual images and erotic website visits that enthralled his curiosity the past few months. He had assumed incognito mode and switching Safari settings to private browsing would hide the salacious content pulling him deeper each night... But here sat his dad ready to lower the boom.

"Dad, I'm so sorry," Justin muttered, face flaming crimson". I don't know why I started looking at that stuff. I guess boredom or stress... But honestly it gripped me. I know I shouldn't have given into temptation." He shook his head regretfully. "I feel so disgusted with my weakness damaging my integrity and witness."

His dad's sternness melted into sadness seeing his son's remorse. "Son, I wish you had come to me sooner so we could fight this battle together. But dwelling on shame or blaming yourself won't solve it. Let's team up setting some boundaries to resist the traps the world lays for curious minds..."

Walk of Freedom

What followed was a raw heart-to-heart talk about guarding eyes from images that demean God's daughters and sons. Justin's dad emphasized that bouncing the eyes to avoid lustful triggers honored God's high design for sexuality rather than repressing natural appetites. He suggested more constructive outlets for energy like sports and creative pursuits to avoid wandering online out of boredom.

Together they installed robust filters on devices and discussed practical strategies to maintain self-control. His dad offered to check in nightly to circumvent mindless web surfing in vulnerable evening hours. He also connected Justin with a mentor for weekly chats about walking in freedom.

"I want you to view me as an ally, not enemy...Your integrity matters more than punitive extremes right now," Justin's dad said. "This may be a tough battle, but Jesus promises the Spirit to empower righteousness. Let's draw on Him to walk this out."

They closed praying for aligned desires and accountable community to steer Justin's conduct into honorable manhood. Both committed to ongoing candid dialogue about combatting lust with grace and truth. Shielding Heart from Lust

Parenting teenagers today can feel like an unending battle against sexual temptations. Lustful traps await around every corner, from provocative selfies to pornography. Youth are told that "sex positivity" and "exploring desires" are not harmful.

As Christian parents, we understand that embracing purity necessitates vigilance. The Bible instructs us to "flee youthful lusts" and to make "no provision for the flesh." Romans 13:14; 2 Timothy 2:22. We can equip teens to guard their hearts against lust with prayerful discipline and God's help.

Let's look at some practical strategies for limiting tempting exposure, developing internal mental filters, and surrounding kids with grace and accountability. While the world says "anything goes," we must teach teenagers to be distinct disciples.

Monitoring Media Choices

Monitoring entertainment choices is critical in today's sexualized media environment. But don't just limit the content. Explain how it can shape desires as well. Set boundaries with intent:

- **Music:** Lyrics glorifying sex, drugs, and partying corrupt the minds of children. Choose performers who are Christian or family-friendly. Talk about the messages in popular songs.
- **Movies/TV:** For graphic content, advance screening is required. Use ratings wisely and be familiar with media themes.

- **Games:** Keep an eye out for chat features and avatars that depict violence, gore, sexuality, or the occult. Set time constraints and accessibility.

- **Books:** Don't take reading for granted. Examine young adult novels, which frequently contain explicit material.

- **Social media:** Follow/friend your teen on social media to monitor content, images, and influencers. Make sure your privacy settings are strict.

- **YouTube/Podcasts:** This site is rife with predatory or age-inappropriate content. View videos, channels, and hosts in advance.

- **Websites:** Use filtering and monitoring to prevent access to inappropriate websites. Place computers in high-traffic areas.

Ongoing communication is also essential. Inquire, for example, "How did that movie represent women?" "What message did that song promote about intimacy?" Discuss the depicted realities versus false fantasies. Deconstruct worldly attitudes that fuel lust.

Setting Internal Filters

Keeping your eyes and ears open is a good place to start. External vigilance, however, is insufficient in a sensual world. Youth require internal mental filters to protect themselves from lust.

However, don't just say, "Don't look!" Teach active strategies such as:

- Silently quote scripture, such as Psalm 101:3, to focus the mind.
- When tempted, immediately divert your gaze and thoughts.
- Refrain from lingering on sensual images. Deprive yourself of the temptation.
- Capture lustful imaginations, reject them, and replace them with spiritual thoughts when they arise. Do not entertain or dwell on sinful fantasies.
- pose the question "would Jesus be pleased with this thought?" Allow righteous shame to motivate a change of course.

Internet access can be restricted using accountability software. However, children require mental discipline to control where their minds wander. Give them tools to redirect their thoughts and capture lustful ones. Make mental shortcuts, such as WWJD bracelets.

Vigilantly discipline their thought lives. Our brains are wired in response to what we feed them over time. Assist teens in feeding their pure minds.

Combating Pornography

Pornography is one of today's most addictive and widespread threats. Parents must be proactive rather than naive. Assume that children will notice it and assist them in developing defenses:

- On all devices, install filters and monitoring software. There will be no unrestricted access or deletions.
- Keep screens in high-traffic areas where they can be seen.

- Configure a time limit password after which devices will lock.

- Look for deleted search histories, cached files, and cookies.

- Make it clear that pornography viewing will not be tolerated in your home. Determine the consequences.

- Discuss the objectification of pornography versus genuine intimacy. Dispel myths about how it will not affect relationships or women's views.

- Examine the underlying vulnerabilities that may make porn more appealing, such as loneliness, stress, low self-esteem, or perfectionism. Better coping strategies and support systems are available.

- Encourage young people to immediately confess their pornographic behavior and seek accountability. Otherwise, it will only take place in secret. So, they keep coming back, offer empathy rather than judgment.

If your teen is already addicted, seek assistance from counselors who specialize in overcoming porn addiction. Hearts can be completely retrained with prayer and determination.

Avoiding Solo Play

Another difficult topic that many parents avoid is masturbation. However, in today's open culture of "self-love," it must be addressed.

- Recognize that masturbation is common, but explain God's design for marital sexuality. Self-gratification can become addictive and distort this sacred purpose.

- Warn about the potential for escalation from mental images to pornography. A destructive cycle is easily established.

- Discuss how masturbation can lead to shame, unhealthy obsessions, and later influence real-life intimacy.

- Oppose the secular view that it is simply "normal exploration." Our bodies are not our own as disciples called apart. Corinthians 6:19-20

- Arm yourself with strategies such as prayer, scripture memory, avoiding idleness, exercise, and wholesome hobbies.

The key is to teach teens that masturbation is contrary to God's purpose for intimacy, rather than just a harmless physical release. Encourage a desire for holy discipline over momentary gratification.

Role Models and Same-Sex Friendships

Strong same-sex friendships help channel attraction and temptation trajectories positively during puberty. Teens should be directed to:

- Make friends with similar values rather than those who pressure them to conform to the world.

- Establish mentoring relationships with godly role models such as youth pastors, relatives, family friends, and so on.

- Join same-gender small groups to find support while pursuing sexual purity and walking closely with Christ.

Our social circles shape us, for better or worse. Invest in mentoring relationships that promote spiritual growth.

Practical Tips: Temptation Triggers

Investigate common "weak spots" that teens may encounter. Create counter-strategies in advance:

a. Set a pickup time for parties. Check in by phone. Avoid unsupervised mingling or overnight stays.

b. Dating: Only meet in public places. There is no alone time at home. Discuss openly the boundaries of intimacy.

c. Online friends: Don't meet up with internet-only friends by yourself. Ask questions and be cautious.

d. Stress and loneliness: Offer healthy outlets such as activity clubs, family time, youth groups, and so on.

e. Tiredness and boredom: Promote productive hobbies over idle web surfing. In your own life, model strategies for renewing energy and variety.

Remove all excuses and opportunities for prey. Help fill needs for connection by uplifting the community rather than providing quick escape routes. Keep an eye out for emotional red flags as well.

Godly Guidance, not Shame

When discussing lust and temptation, make sure that the motivation is reverence for God rather than shame. Explain:

a. Avoiding lust pleases God, who knows that His boundaries protect us rather than deprive us.

b. Maintaining control over our thoughts and actions honors God's temple in our bodies.

c. Saving intimacy for marriage gives that gift to a future spouse completely.

The goal is not to feel guilty, but to embrace God's protective design for passion. We honor Him by exercising restraint.

Responding Gracefully

Teens will make mistakes despite their best efforts. When they reveal difficulties:

a. Express forgiveness, empathy, and help.

b. Point them to Bible verses about redemption, such as Romans 3:23 and Proverbs 28:13.

c. Avoid shaming, but instead discuss constructive boundaries/accountability in the future.

d. Seek professional help if addiction-level patterns emerge.

e. Remind them that their worth has not diminished, but that God has better plans for them.

f. Make a commitment to increasing monitoring and mentoring efforts.

Pitfalls, with God's help, can strengthen character and deepen reliance on Him. Allow your home to be a refuge of grace as we all grow in Christ.

Question and Answer for Chapter 4

Q: Why do I have sexual urges and thoughts even though I'm not married? Isn't that wrong?

A: Those desires are normal, but acting on them through masturbation or sex outside marriage goes against God's plan. He wants us to control our bodies in holiness and honor (1 Thess. 4:3-5). Let's talk about positive ways to channel those urges.

Q: What's wrong with watching pornography if it doesn't hurt anyone?

A: Pornography objectifies people and can warp healthy sexuality. It often leads to addiction too. God calls us to dwell on what's pure (Philippians 4:8). Let's set limits on devices to avoid temptation traps.

Q: My friends are sharing inappropriate photos and jokes. How do I stay cool without participating?

A: Peer pressure is so hard! But the Bible says bad company corrupts good character (1 Cor. 15:33). Let's talk to your youth pastor for strategies on relating to friends positively while setting boundaries.

Q: I keep struggling with temptation and failing. Is something wrong with me?

A: Not at all! Even heroes of the faith like David faced sexual temptation. Through Christ, we can reset our minds and start fresh. Let's read God's promises of restoration together. Staying connected in Christian community is key too.

Q: How far is too far physically before marriage?

A: Anything stirring up arousal like passionate kissing, touching private areas, sharing beds, etc. can lead to losing self-control. Let's talk about setting some boundaries to save special intimacies for your future spouse.

CHAPTER FIVE

Navigating Gender Identity and Sexuality

As mom of three Vivian pulled into the high school driveway, she braced for what awaited after the phone call... Her 16-year-old daughter siting tearfully with the principal for refusing to use a transgender classmate's preferred pronoun.

While Vivian understood Emma's biblical convictions, she dreaded hearing how her response came across to fragile peers. Emma was an empathetic ally, not a bigot. Yet complex gender conversations required balancing grace and truth delicately in this politically charged climate.

Vivian prayed under her breath, "Lord, grant me wisdom guiding Emma to stand by truth without sacrificing sensitivity... help my words bring life!"

She entered determined to listen before reacting, seeking to understand all sides despite personal views. But Vivian knew she couldn't leave Emma without prayerful counsel on articulating biblical beliefs gently amid opposing cultural tides...

Understanding Struggles

Inside Principal Ryan's office, Emma sat slumped with red-rimmed eyes while a blonde student Vivian presumed was the offended classmate centered defiantly.

"Mrs. Clark, thanks for coming on short notice," Principal Ryan said solemnly as Vivian took a seat beside Emma who wouldn't meet her gaze. "As you can see, we had an incident where Emma referred to student Leslie here by her former male name and pronouns. Leslie understandably felt hurt, while Emma claims constitutional freedoms should protect her speech."

He glanced between the two girls sympathetically. "I aim to facilitate open dialogue, not attacks from either camp. Can we share perspectives considering where everyone is coming from?"

Over the next hour, Leslie described long feeling "trapped in the wrong body," wrestling confusion compounded by an absent father andbullies mocking "sissy" mannerisms growing up. Transitioning brought relief, she tearfully explained. When Emma "misgendered" her, painful rejection resurfaced.

In response, Emma appealed to her biblical worldview of humans created male and female, designed intentionally by a loving God. "While I cannot understand Leslie's pain," she offered gently "my belief holds that rejecting or altering one's biological sex violates God's plan. I want to show grace without affirming what my faith teaches is untrue. But I'm sincerely sorry for hurting you..."

Leslie huffed in response. "Don't force your religion on me! You may not agree with who I am, but respect demands using my chosen pronoun or else it's violence!"

Seeking Reconciliation

Principal Ryan mediates some compromise around avoiding outright misgendering, while allowing Emma to use Leslie's name without pronouns if possible. He pledged to revisit school transgender policies soon.

In the aftermath, Vivian reassured a distraught Emma that showing uncompromising grace reflects Jesus' heart. "You stood by truth yet apologized for pain caused. I'm proud of you for doing both with poise."

She explained God's design of male and female but lamented church history of marginalizing those identifying as LGBTQ. "Pray to discern where conviction should remain firm versus adapting language or tactics so no one feels condemned as we build bridges sharing truth."

They discussed lessons moving forward about refusing "enemies" labels for peers struggling with their identity and past pains. Vivian urged Emma to extend compassion while standing confidently in her biblical convictions when challenged.

"My prayer is you'll avoid hostility on all sides to become a bridge-builder. We don't glorify God by affirming LGBTQ theology as biblical nor maligning their humanity as fallen shorts of straightness. There's light exposing darkness if we walk in grace as Christ..."

As cultural flashpoints arise, Vivian keeps discipling Emma with that vision central. If she can shape prayers more than protests, spur faith fragrant with grace beyond moral outrage, seeds of restoration may yet yield a harvest through Emma's voice echoing timeless truth paired with unconditional belonging.

Understanding Homosexuality

How do you respond if your child enquires about homosexuality or same-sex relationships? Begin by asking gentle questions to understand their point of view and the experiences that piqued their interest. Confirm your interest in complex issues.

Then explain how the Bible teaches that God created sex to unite male and female in committed marriage. While cultures promote a variety of viewpoints, God makes it clear that homosexuality is not in His design:

1. "God created man in His own image, in the image of God He created him; male and female He created them." (See Genesis 1:27)

2. "As a result, God gave them over to dishonorable passions." For their women exchanged natural relations for those that are contrary to nature, and the men likewise gave up natural relations with women and were consumed with passion for one another, men committing shameless acts with men and receiving the due penalty for their error in themselves." (1 Corinthians 1:26-27)

Make it clear that you do not pass judgment or condemnation on anyone. At times, we all struggle with desires that are contrary to God's will. However, obedience entails giving up our identities and passions when they conflict with God's loving boundaries for life and intimacy.

Use age-appropriate language while adhering to the standards of Scripture. God's plan isn't always easy, but it's always for our benefit.

Loving Others Without Affirming Sin

A key message is the distinction between love for the person and approval of sinful lifestyles. When children have LGBTQ classmates and friends, teach them how to demonstrate God's love:

a. Show respect to everyone. Do not bully, mock, or use derogatory language.

b. Be welcoming and caring to LGBTQ students. Get to know them on a personal level.

c. Speak up for them if they are mistreated or mocked by others.

d. Ask God to open their hearts to God's truth.

e. Look for common interests to form genuine friendships.

f. Answer questions about your faith in a humble manner. Do not debate or pontificate.

g. When moral issues arise, speak the truth with gentle courage rather than judgment.

The goal is to strike a balance between conviction and compassion. We do not support LGBTQ lifestyles, but we love our neighbors as if they were our own.

Handling Struggles with Same-Sex Attraction

If your teen discloses that he or she is experiencing same-sex attraction, respond with love and sensitivity:

1. First, thank them for having the courage and faith to confide in you. Assure them of your undying love. Make it clear to them that you value them for more than their desires or struggles.

2. In order to understand when and how these feelings began, as well as the context surrounding them, ask open-ended questions. Listen without passing judgment.

3. Make it clear that God adores them as His precious child. Assure them that Jesus is aware of the conflict

between desires and God's commands. He has walked in our shoes and gives us the strength to overcome.

4. If your teen complains about ongoing SSA battles, don't say it's "just a phase." Empathize with how painful and isolating it must be.

5. Pray for each other's strength, wisdom, and comfort. Don't try conversion therapy. However, encourage them to focus on Christian community, godly relationships, and biblical perspectives on gender, sexuality, and sanctification.

6. Consider seeking professional Christian counseling to address the underlying causes of SSA, such as childhood wounds, emotional dependency issues, a lack of same-sex parent bonding, sexual abuse, or family dysfunction. Determine whether SSRI medication can help you rebalance your serotonin levels.

Commit to walking patiently with your teen through the process, even if it is confusing or painful for you. Your unwavering love and grace are a reflection of the Father's heart.

Navigating Transgender Identity Issues

Gender dysphoria and transgender identity cause significant confusion in Christian children. Young children may inadvertently act out gender roles. However, if a teen declares that they believe they are the opposite sex, a thoughtful response is required.

First, express your gratitude and love for their trust in you. Take the time to listen to and comprehend their story without becoming emotionally involved. Pose sensitive questions:

- When did you start feeling this way?
- What makes you feel you identify as (opposite gender)?

- How long have you felt like you were trapped in the wrong body?
- What steps have you taken so far to align with your identity? Have you told anyone else?

Avoid exclamations such as "You're too young to know!" Confirm their willingness to share. Also express your desire to learn more in order to fully comprehend the situation.

Next, explain how God purposefully created each person, whether male or female, for divine purposes:

"So, God created man in his own image, in the image of God he created him; male and female he created them." (See Genesis 1:27)

While transgender identity is becoming more popular, God's truth remains constant. In counseling, request openness to further investigate His design and biblical gender ethics.

If your teen insists on being the opposite sex, don't give in to requests for hormones, wardrobe changes, or new pronouns right away. These reinforce identity confusion. Delay such actions lovingly while seeking professional Christian counseling.

Allowing emotional maturity and biblical counsel to dispel what is frequently a passing phase influenced by cultural trends, mental health issues, abuse, or misunderstandings about God's intent is the goal. Confirm God's intentions in their birth gender.

Most of the time, it will not be simple or quick. However, with prayer and patience, children experiencing gender dysphoria can find wholeness in their God-given identity.

Standing Firm with Truth and Grace

Our hypersexualized culture will continue to push for the normalization of all expressions. As Christ's disciples, we must not compromise biblical truths, but rather hold them gently, speaking truth with the same grace that we want for our own flaws.

Don't be afraid to confront your children with difficult questions. Have open conversations in which they feel comfortable confiding their innermost struggles. Listen without passing judgment as you point them to the perfect design of the Father for restoring beautiful identity and purpose.

We can equip the next generation to walk out God's plan for sexuality and relationships with boldness and compassion if we use the Bible as our source and prayer as our strength. Our world requires light to shine brightly and draw prodigal's home.

Question and Answer for Chapter 5

Q: My friend has two dads who are married. Why is that wrong? They seem like nice people.

A: The Bible shows God designed marriage for one man and one woman (Genesis 2:24). Any sexual relationship outside that is considered sinful. We should be kind to others without supporting lifestyles the Bible calls immoral. Let's pray for wisdom to balance both grace and truth.

Q: Why does our church not allow gay people to get married or be leaders? Isn't that discrimination?

A: God's word prohibits homosexual practice, not people. We want everyone to feel welcome while holding church roles and sacraments as God designed them. It's difficult in today's culture, so we must show empathy while clinging to what scripture states.

Q: What should I do if my friend tells me they are transgender?

A: Listen with compassion and don't condemn struggles you may not relate to. But avoid affirming false gender identities not aligned with their biological sex. God lovingly crafted each of us as male or female (Genesis 1:27). Continue inviting them into Christian community for support walking in God's truth.

Q: Is it sinful for me to have attractions or thoughts about someone of my same gender?

A: Not necessarily. Many people face fleeting confused feelings or temptations out of their control. Dwelling on fantasies or experimenting can lead to sin though. Let's talk through these emotions from a biblical perspective. Staying anchored in scripture and accountability will keep you on the right path.

CHAPTER SIX

Protecting Innocence

Joanna and Trevor taught their 8-year-old daughter Hannah about protecting her body and reporting unwanted touch from a young age. Hannah's uncle Evan recently tickled her thighs and butt during roughhousing at a family gathering. She was uneasy, but she wasn't sure what to say because he was a close relative.

Hannah approached her mother with trepidation that night. "I have something to tell you. Uncle Evan's hands went somewhere they shouldn't have when he was tickling me today."

Joanna kept her voice down and thanked Hannah for sharing. She assured her that she had done the right thing and that it was not her fault. Before contacting authorities, she asked enough questions to determine the nature of the contact.

Trevor praised his daughter for speaking up. "I admire you for telling us. You defended yourself and can help prevent bad behavior." He reassured her that she would not be in any trouble.

Joanna and Trevor used age-appropriate language to explain how Evan violated body boundaries and how the police would handle the situation. They prayed together for God's comfort, wisdom, and justice.

Hannah's parents sought professional counseling to help her deal with any feelings of shame or confusion. They assured her that, despite someone else's sin, she was still perfectly innocent and precious in God's eyes.

Hannah was relieved that her parents believed her and acted quickly. Because they had instilled courage in her from a young age, she spoke up before the abuse escalated. Her confidence enabled them to intervene and prevent further harm.

Safeguarding Against Predators

As parents, we treasure our children's wide-eyed innocence. Unfortunately, dangerous predators want to take advantage of that purity. According to statistics, 1 in 9 girls and 1 in 53 boys are sexually abused before the age of 18.

As Christian parents, we must be aware of potential dangers, empower children to report inappropriate contact, and assist young victims in finding healing in Christ. While we cannot protect the lambs God entrusts to us from all evil in this fallen world, we can help to protect them.

Starting Early with Body Safety Rules

The best defense begins with teaching children about body safety at a young age. Set guidelines and use proper anatomy terminology:

- God created your body to be unique. It should be treated as a temple.
- Your private parts are only visible and touchable by you.
- If anyone tries to see or touch them, say "No!" and immediately notify Mommy or Daddy.
- Doctors or parents may need to examine your body in order for it to remain healthy. However, no one else should.
- Always ask before hugging. If you are uncomfortable, say no.
- Inform Mommy or Daddy if you see pictures or videos of naked people.
- Never allow adults to ask you to keep secrets from Mommy and Daddy.

To demonstrate these principles, use age-appropriate books or videos. Act out scenarios such as saying no to inappropriate touching and immediately informing your parents. Make it clear that they will not "get in trouble" for reporting concerns. Only the adult who is wrong will face consequences.

Instilling Boldness, Not Fear

The goal is not to instill fear in children, but to encourage them to speak up. Avoid ominous cautions such as "Don't take candy from strangers!" This perplexes children. Instead, provide specific instructions such as:

- If anyone threatens you with "Don't tell or else..." tell Mommy and Daddy right away.
- Except for doctors with a parent present, no adult should touch your private parts.
- If someone attempts to force affection or touch you in a private area, yell "Stop it!" and tell us what happened.

- You will not be punished if you say "no" to inappropriate touching or report it to us. We'll keep you safe.

Make it clear to children that you are a safe haven. Never shame them if they report abuse; instead, applaud their bravery in speaking up. Implement child protection policies in collaboration with your church.

Identifying Grooming Behaviors

Before acting, predators use deceptive tactics such as grooming to gain trust. Teach children to spot deception:

- Experiment with boundaries by telling sexual jokes or showing images to see how they react.

- Making a child's acquaintance through games, treats, outings, compliments, sharing "secrets," and so on.
- Touching that gradually crosses into private areas
- Isolating a child from peers or other adults who may notice unusual behavior.

- Endangering or bribing a child in order to prevent disclosure

Make children aware that predators may pose as friends while secretly violating boundaries. Insist that uncomfortable touching be reported even if the person is otherwise pleasant.

Monitoring the Safety of Older Children

Don't assume that predators only prey on children. Teens are also groomed by older boyfriends/girlfriends, mentors, coaches, and so on. Discuss the following red flags to look for in older children's relationships:

- An older romantic partner who keeps them away from family and friends
- Someone who insists on keeping the relationship private.
- Rapidly developing physical intimacy
- Disruptive behavior or abusive language
- Giving them gifts or money as a form of coercion
- Unauthorized photography or videography

- Allowing them to be exposed to alcohol, drugs, or pornography

Discuss openly what healthy dating entails and entails— mutual respect, self-control, limits, and family awareness. Make it clear to teens that you are available to them if they have any relationship concerns.

Take action if you have concerns, even if your teen dismisses them. Don't hold out for proof or complete disclosure. If necessary, intervene through police and counselors to establish safety and wise boundaries.

Healing Abuse Through Counseling

If you discover that your child has been abused, take the following steps:

- State unequivocally that it was not their fault. Do not point fingers or obsess over minor details. Just enough to report on.

- Contact the police immediately and discontinue contact with the perpetrator.

- Seek professional counseling to assist your child in processing emotions such as shame, anger, and betrayal.

- Join hands in prayer for healing. Scriptures about God's love and promises for their lives should be read aloud.

- Gently reassure them that they are still innocent, loved, and precious.

- Don't put pressure on them to "get over it." Be patient as the counseling process unfolds.

- Seek counseling for yourself as well. Coping strategies are required when assisting victims of abuse.

- Inquire with counselors about how to maintain healthy relationships and boundaries in the future.

Your child can be restored by grace with time, counseling, and God's redemption. While innocence can be stolen, hope can never be.

Protecting Within the Church

Unfortunately, the majority of abuse occurs within trusted circles such as family and church. Policies to protect children are critical:

- Require background checks for all employees and volunteers who work with children.
- Require workers to receive abuse prevention training.
- Adults should not be alone with minors without supervision.

- Make sure children understand where they can report concerns about leaders' behavior.
- Respond quickly to any allegations and notify authorities.
- Provide pastoral care to victims and their families.

No system is immune to abuse. However, adhering to standards reduces risks and increases reporting power.

Keeping Watch Through Prayer

In the end, only God can fully protect children. As Christian parents, He allows us to be His hands, eyes, and voice on earth. We can:

- Request that the Holy Spirit alert us to any signs indicating a threat to our child's safety or purity. Sharpen our ability to detect predatory behavior in adults who interact with our children.

- Request a supernatural shield of protection for our children (Job 1:10).

- Pray for hearts to be healed of past abuse, so that shame is replaced by God's grace and truth.

- Request that God protect innocent minds and bodies from sexualized content, images, and suggestions.

May we take every precaution while putting our trust in God for what we cannot control. Let us protect the youngest among us not only with vigilance, but also with patient faith in the Good Shepherd's faithful care.

Question and Answer for Chapter 6

Q: My uncle asks me to keep special secrets when he takes me places alone. Is that okay?

A: Adults should never ask kids to keep secrets from parents - that's very wrong. Please tell me if anyone says this, so I can make sure you stay safe. I'm so glad you asked me about this!

Q: My coach gives me extra gifts and attention. I feel weird but don't want to get him in trouble. What should I do?

A: This sounds very concerning. Let me know exactly what gifts or special attention he shows you - that could be grooming behavior. I promise you won't get in trouble for telling. We need to speak up to protect you!

Q: If I report abuse, what will happen? Will it mess up my family?

A: You did the right thing by reporting! Sadly abuse tears families apart but getting you help is most important. This was not your fault at all. Let's pray and I'll support you through the process of finding healing.

Q: How can I tell the difference between safe touch vs. wrong touch?

A: Safe touch is about caring - gentle hugs from family, high-fives with friends, mom kissing a hurt elbow. Wrong touch involves private zones God calls us to cover. Pay attention to any touch making you feel uneasy. You can always tell me if something confuses or bothers you.

Q: Why would someone touch a child in a dangerous way?

A: Sometimes people have problems in their minds or hearts that lead them to harm others. It's very sad. But that's why it's so important you tell me about any wrong touching right away so we can get help. I'm proud of you for asking me questions!

CONCLUSION

What a journey it's been walking through God's perspective on shaping kids' sexual ethics! Over the past chapters, we've explored laying a strong foundation in modesty and self-respect early on, navigating puberty changes through the lens of our identity in Christ, guarding innocent hearts against worldly temptations, and preparing teens to embrace sexuality within marriage.

I pray these practical tips spur many open, honest and grace-filled conversations in your family for years to come.

While it hasn't been easy countering cultural lies at times, you as parents have diligently sowed seeds of truth, discretion and holiness in the fertile soil of your children's hearts. As the saying goes "as the twig is bent, so grows the tree." The habits and values established today will bear much fruit in stronger marriages and deeper intimacy tomorrow.

But our journey is far from over. The pre-teen or tween years usher in whole new dynamics. Raging hormones, peer pressures and turbulent emotions will challenge convictions like never before. As our kids stand on the cusp of young adulthood, the world shouts louder than ever to throw off moral restraint.

Yet, we must double down on discipleship with even more grace and wisdom. Continue seeking teachable moments to reinforce God's beautiful design amidst their questions, struggles and pain. Some days they'll push back hard, testing boundaries like all adolescents do as independence awakens. But don't lose heart. With prayer and unconditional love, these temporary growing pains lead to maturity in Christ.

Navigating the Coming Years

While every child develops differently, you can expect new dynamics as your sons and daughters enter the teen years.

Here's an overview of key topics to expect addressing more in-depth down the road:

Early Teen (Ages 12-14):

- Continuing "puberty talks" as new changes unfold
- Establishing technology boundaries as independence increases.
- Discussing healthy boundaries for budding romantic interest
- Reinforcing identity in Christ despite social challenges
- Ongoing conversations about God's design for sexuality amid changing societal views

Mid-Teen (Ages 15-17):

- Equipping teens to guard their hearts against pornography and sexual experimentation
- Coaching wise decision-making about intimacy in dating relationships
- Helping teens set physical limits in romantic contexts

- Discussing LGBTQ complexities with biblical truth and compassion
- Preparing for conversations about sexual ethics with future spouses

Late Teen (Ages 18-19):

- Affirming their growth into godly manhood and womanhood
- Discussing hormones, arousal and intimacy in marriage openly
- Equipping them to spot and stop sexual predation in college/workplace
- Affirming saving sex for the wedding night without shame
- Celebrating their transition into independent and wise adulthood

More Conversations to Come

I hope this gives a small glimpse into the road ahead. While today's cultural climate presents growing challenges, remember "He who began a good work will carry it onto completion" (Philippians 1:6). Continue reinforcing the biblical foundations laid to uphold God's design for flourishing families in generations to come.

And if stumbles occur along the way, respond in grace, reestablishing holy boundaries. Our kids need compassionate mentors, not condemners, no matter what temptations or questions they face.

Stay alert to new peer pressures and media influences to address. But trust God to cement their identity in Christ above all else. His truths and boundaries remain steadfast however much our world may drift.

As the father promises in Isaiah 54:13, "All your children will be taught by the Lord, and great will be their peace."

May His wisdom and guidance equip your family to embrace all the beauty, wonder and responsibility of passing on Godly sexual ethics for generations to come!

APPENDIX

Further Learning for Parents:

- Every Young Man's Battle: Strategies for Victory in the Real World of Sexual Temptation by Stephen Arterburn and Fred Stoeker

- The Comprehensive Illustrated Body Guide for Girls Ages 8 To 12 Year Olds: A Guide to Understanding Puberty, Periods, and Sex Education. Everything Your ... and Caring for Her Body by Sonya Dunham

- Passport2Purity Kit by Dennis and Barbara Rainey (materials and getaway guide to connect with your preteen)

- Good Pictures, Bad Pictures: Porn-Proofing Today's Young Kids by Kristen Jenson

- 31 Days to Masculinity: Helping Boys Become Confident, Courageous Young Men by Douglas Wilson

Youth Curriculums and Education:

- The Talk: 7 Lessons to Introduce Your Child to Biblical Sexuality by Luke Gilkerson

- Coming of Age by Evangelical Child and Family Agency (ECFA)

- Life on Track - Biblical Sexuality for Students by Scott Bussjaeger, LMFT

Websites:

- CovenantEyes.com (Internet filtering and accountability)
- Focus on the Family's Kids of Integrity (Family discipleship tools)
- ProtectYoungMinds.org (Preventing child exposure to pornography)
- Axis.org (Help for teens struggling with sexuality/porn addiction)

- FreedomInMind.com (Exodus from LGBTQ lifestyle)

Counselor Referral Networks:

- AACC's Find a Counselor tool (Christian counseling for pornography, same-sex attraction, etc)

- NCOSE's National Sexual Exploitation Treatment Provider Directory (Certified Sex Addiction Therapists)

Let these additional faith-based programs, tools and professionals aid you along the journey. This is not a comprehensive list, but provides reputable resources for digging deeper. Let's help our kids thrive in God's loving design for sexuality!

64126054R00076